HELPING KIDS GET ORGANIZED

Activities that Teach Time Management, Clutter Clearing, Project Planning, and More!

By Robyn Freedman Spizman and
Marianne Daniels Garber, Ph.D.

Illustrated by Corbin Hillam

Good Apple
An imprint of Paramount Supplemental Education

Executive Editor: Carolea Williams
Editor: Christine Hood
Inside Design: Rose Sheifer and Ginny Coull
Cover Design: Marek/Janci

ISBN 0-86653-840-2

Printed in the United States of America
1. 9 8 7 6 5 4 3 2 1

Contents

Introduction

Very few of us are naturally organized individuals. We must all learn effective ways to approach and complete various tasks. Unfortunately, most of us are so busy that it takes years to realize there might have been an easier way to complete most of the work we've accomplished.

The purpose of this book is to prepare students for learning by teaching them effective organizational habits—how to approach a task, organize a workspace, divide an assignment into manageable goals, and effectively complete a project in a timely manner.

Each activity progressively moves students towards developing good study and work habits. Students begin by recognizing the needs and benefits of being organized and end with planning for major projects and setting long-term goals. And, since maintenance is the key to long-lasting organization, students will learn how to maintain the skills they develop.

Reproducible rewards and certificates are included to provide a means of recognizing and rewarding your students' increasing progress towards organization. By learning how to organize effectively, your students will become masters of time management and approach assignments, tests, and projects with complete confidence.

Name _____

Clean Up!

 **Target messy areas as a first step towards developing organizational skills.**

Circle every area on this page that is out of control and filled with clutter. Then describe how you would organize or clean up each mess in the space below.

How would you clean up this clutter?

_____

_____

_____

_____

Organizing Your Environment

Helping Kids Get Organized © 1995 Good Apple

Clutter Control

 **Find out which organizational skills you already possess and which you need to develop.**

Are you sloppy or super organized? Take this test to determine how much mess is getting in your way. Circle 4 if the statement is always true, 3 if it is often true, 2 if it is sometimes true, 1 if it occasionally true, and 0 if it is never true. Add up all the circled numbers to get your final score.

1. I remember to bring my homework to school.   0 1 2 3 4
2. I plan for big projects in advance.   0 1 2 3 4
3. I bring everything I need for my assignments to school every day.   0 1 2 3 4
4. I have a special place to study at home.   0 1 2 3 4
5. I have a dictionary, a good light, and study tools at home.   0 1 2 3 4
6. My homework environment is quiet and undisturbed.   0 1 2 3 4
7. I check to be sure I have my assignments before leaving school.   0 1 2 3 4
8. My room is neat and everything has a place.   0 1 2 3 4
9. My homework assignments are very neat.   0 1 2 3 4
10. At the beginning of each week, I think about what I need to accomplish.   0 1 2 3 4
11. When I have a major project due, I plan how I will get it accomplished and mark tasks on a calendar.   0 1 2 3 4
12. I plan ahead so I won't have to stay up late cramming for tests.   0 1 2 3 4
13. I keep my desk at school uncluttered and orderly.   0 1 2 3 4

Total your points.
40+   Excellent! Keep up the good work.
27-39   You're on your way. Keep working.
14-26   You have some work to do.
0-13   You need to take some big steps to improve your habits.

Name _____

Messy Desk Blues

 **Keep your desk neat and organized so you can find items when you need them.**

This desk is a disaster! Check this desk thoroughly and circle everything that doesn't belong.

Check your own desk. Is it neat and tidy or does it need some organizing? Describe how it is different or similar to the desk pictured above.

_____

_____

_____

_____

_____

Organizing Your Environment

Name _____

Organize Your Desk

 **Keep everything you need for your daily classroom activities in a special place so you can find them easily and quickly.**

It's not enough to have the right materials and study tools. You must be able to find what you need when you need it. It is helpful to have a special place to keep your tools. Where do you keep your pencils and erasers? Are your notebooks and papers in order or are they disorganized and scattered? Do you keep food in your desk?

On the left side of the page, draw the contents of your desk the way it is now. On the right side, design a plan for organizing your desk. Include "must have" objects.

Name _____

Help Keep Your Classroom Organized

 Help keep your classroom organized to create a better learning environment for everyone.

What is your classroom environment like? Do you help to keep book shelves tidy? Do you help straighten stacks of paper, empty the pencil sharpener, and keep supplies in good order?

Complete a drawing of your classroom below. Include items such as your desk, your teacher's desk, the chalkboard, book shelves, encyclopedias, and maps. Place an X over areas in the classroom that you can help keep tidy and organized.

Describe how you will help make your classroom a more organized place to learn.

_____

_____

_____

_____

Helping Kids Get Organized © 1995 Good Apple

Name _____

Go For it and Get Organized

Take a walk around your house. Look in each room, the garage, and even out in the yard. List every area which needs your special organizing touch and describe how you might approach some of these tasks. Try to accomplish one task each week, either by yourself or with a parent or sibling.

1. _____
I will organize this by

_____

_____

_____

4. _____
I will organize this by

_____

_____

_____

2. _____
I will organize this by

_____

_____

_____

5. _____
I will organize this by

_____

_____

_____

3. _____
I will organize this by

_____

_____

_____

6. _____
I will organize this by

_____

_____

_____

Name _____

Avoid Closet Chaos

 **Always put your clothing back where it belongs to avoid closet chaos.**

Your closet is a great place to get organized. Begin by trying on everything in your closet. If it fits, keep it. If it doesn't, consult with your parent(s) and decide where the outgrown clothing will go. Organize your clothing in a way that makes everything easy to locate and stick to the system. You could group your clothes by colors or place all the shirts together, pants together, and so on.

Explain how you organized your closet.

_____

_____

_____

_____

Illustrate your newly organized closet.

Helping Kids Get Organized © 1995 Good Apple

Name _____

Tools of the Trade

> ✏️ **Make sure you have the right kinds of study tools at school and at home.**

You should be aware of tools you need every day and those you only need occasionally for special projects. For example, for this activity you will need a red, green, and blue pen or marker.

Draw a red circle around the tools you need every day to do your assignments at school or home. Underline with blue the items you need a few times a week. Draw a green rectangle around the items you only need once in a while.

notebook paper	compass	pencils
dictionary	scissors	eraser
blank paper	protractor	crayons
thesaurus	ruler	ink pen
graph paper	file folders	colored pencils
encyclopedia	paper clips	typewriter
index cards	computer	markers
tape	stapler	calendar
construction paper	calculator	red pen

Make a list of the "must have" items below. Check your list against the items you have in your desk or at home.

_____

_____

_____

_____

Identifying and Using Study Tools

What Tools Do I Need?

 **Have the right kinds of study tools for your assignments handy.**

Knowing what you need to complete a task is half the work. Using the wrong reference source or the wrong tool can make twice as much work for you.

Identify the tools you will need to complete each of the tasks listed below. Tools may be used more than once and several may be listed for each task.

Example:
Measure your height _____C_____

1. Attach several pages together _____
2. Measure the angle of a triangle _____
3. Write the rough draft of a story _____
4. Determine the pronunciation of a word _____
5. Draw a circle _____
6. Find a synonym for a word _____
7. Write the final draft of a story _____
8. Draw a straight line _____
9. Determine how many days before a report is due _____
10. Gather information about George Washington _____
11. Proofread a paper _____
12. Find the meaning of a word _____
13. Make a cover for a book report _____
14. Figure out the answer to a math problem _____
15. Organize book notes for a research project _____
16. Find the capital of India _____
17. Organize assignments by subject _____

a. compass
b. eraser
c. ruler
d. paper clips
e. index cards
f. stapler
g. scissors
h. calculator
i. pencils
j. computer
k. typewriter
l. dictionary
m. protractor
n. file folders
o. thesaurus
p. calendar
q. tape
r. encyclopedia
s. atlas
t. red pen
u. paper

Identifying and Using Study Tools

Helping Kids Get Organized © 1995 Good Apple

Name _____

File it

 Get in the habit of saving and filing important papers and tests.

Having notes, past tests, and reports organized and handy will help you review for tests and prepare future reports. To create a file, you need to know how to label file folders and in which order to file them. An effective way to file papers is to place them in alphabetical order.

The files below are out of order. Write the file names on the other side of the page in the correct order.

Physical Education   _____

Math   _____

Birthdays   _____

Social Studies   _____

Yearly Calendar   _____

Mr. John Doe   _____

French   _____

The Sleepy Eye Motel   _____

Spanish   _____

Sports   _____

Homework   _____

Spelling   _____

Science   _____

Ms. Jody Miller   _____

Reading   _____

Language Arts   _____

Nutrition   _____

Art Projects   _____

The Windy Mountain Resort   _____

Compositions   _____

Weekly Schedules   _____

Special Projects   _____

My School File

 **Set up your own file system that will help you organize your school work.**

Begin your filing system by finding a box big enough to hold file folders. Create one folder for each course and separate files for special projects or tests. Create a system that works best for you. Clearly label each folder so you can find it easily. You may also want to include extracurricular activities or events, such as birthdays, that you would like to keep in order.

Decide which files you would like to create and fill in the labels below. Make sure you write your file names in the order in which they will actually be filed.

Identifying and Using Study Tools

Helping Kids Get Organized © 1995 Good Apple

Name _____

Get the Jist . . . Make a List

 **Make reminder lists to keep track of the things you need to do.**

Think about the things you need to do and get in the habit of writing them down and making a list. Fill the list on this page with things you need to get done in the next week. Check off each item when you complete it.

Things I need to do!

1 _____
2 _____
3 _____
4 _____
5 _____
6 _____
7 _____
8 _____
9 _____
10 _____

Helping Kids Get Organized © 1995 Good Apple

Name _____

What Kind of Learner Are You?

> Discover the way you learn new information best.

There are several ways people learn and remember new information. "Visual learners" learn best by watching or observing. "Kinesthetic learners" learn best by using their hands and actually constructing projects. The last group is called "auditory learners." These people learn best by listening. Complete this questionnaire to find out what kind of learner you are. Circle one letter in parenthesis in each sentence.

1. When you study printed material, do you prefer to read aloud (A) or read silently (V)?

2. When your teacher gives a lesson, do you remember the content better if he or she lectures (A), performs a demonstration (V), or creates a game requiring class participation (K)?

3. During a lecture, do you learn better when you take notes (K) or just listen quietly (A)?

4. If you could choose how to do a book report, would you rather give an oral report (A), write a report (V), or build a model (K)?

5. Would you rather perform a lab experiment (K) or read about it (V)?

6. Would you rather watch a demonstration (V) or build your own model (K) to learn a concept?

7. When you listen to a lecture for a long time, what do you do to stay focused? Follow along in the book (V), feel the need to talk or discuss (A), or take notes (K)?

8. Do you feel you can best demonstrate what you know when you can show or display something (V), discuss it with someone (A), or write about it (K)?

9. When playing a game, do you understand the rules better if you read them silently to yourself (V), if someone reads them aloud to you (A), or if you start playing and just learn as you go along (K)?

10. Do you learn better through group interaction (A), or alone (V)?

Add up the total number of V's, K's and A's.

If you have more V's, you probably learn best by observing.

If you have mostly K's, you learn best when you are able to do things with your hands.

If most of your answers are A, you learn best by listening.

Developing Effective Homework Habits

Helping Kids Get Organized © 1995 Good Apple

Name _____

Know Your Study Style

 **Identify and understand your study habits.**

Picture yourself studying at home and list everything that is going on around you. Is the radio on? Are brothers or sisters talking to you? Are you eating or watching television? Is it late at night or earlier in the afternoon? Put a star by those things that contribute to your success and a check mark next to those things that distract you.

1. _____
_____

2. _____
_____

3. _____
_____

4. _____
_____

5. _____
_____

6. _____
_____

7. _____
_____

8. _____
_____

Name _____

Zap Distractions

 Find a special place to do your home-work where you will be undisturbed.

What keeps you from studying? Get in a group with three or four of your classmates and discuss the distractions listed below. Check off the ones that disturb you the most and then add to the list. Find a solution for avoiding each distraction.

Distraction	Solution
Stomach growling.	Get a snack.
Younger brother or sister.	
Telephone.	
Television or radio.	
Getting sleepy.	
Pet.	

Developing Effective Homework Habits

Homework in Progress

Sometimes it's hard to get homework done when you are constantly interrupted. Color and cut out this door sign. Hang it on the doorknob of the room in which you study to show others that you are busy with homework.

Name _____

Study Skill Survey

➡ **Develop the study skill of planning ahead.**

See how prepared you are by completing this survey. Check off the items that apply to you. At the bottom of the page, write down a few ideas for improving your study habits.

- [ ] I have all the materials I need at home to get my work done.
- [ ] I have a quiet area with good lighting where I can do my homework.
- [ ] I set aside a specific time each afternoon or evening to complete my studies.
- [ ] I keep an up-to-date assignment book to keep track of what I need to do and how to plan ahead for future projects.
- [ ] I know how to break down a project into several manageable tasks so that I am prepared when the time comes.
- [ ] I listen carefully in class and take notes.
- [ ] I prepare ahead of time for the topics we are studying in class.
- [ ] I underline the main facts when I take notes and know how to identify the most important information.
- [ ] I study my class notes and prepare ahead of time for tests.
- [ ] Before a test, I make sure I have memorized the information correctly.
- [ ] I say the information I need to learn aloud while I write it down to help me remember the answers.
- [ ] I make sure I have extra pencils and erasers ready before a test.
- [ ] I break down reading assignments into sections so it is easier to keep up.

How can you improve your study habits?

_____

_____

_____

_____

Helping Kids Get Organized © 1995 Good Apple

Name _____

Homework Plan

➤ **Designate a special time each day to do your homework.**

It is important to develop a homework plan that works for you. Consider some of your current homework habits. Do you complete your homework as soon as you get home from school or do you take a break before starting work? How long does it usually take you to complete your homework? Do you daydream and take a lot of breaks?

Use this chart to design a homework plan. Think about all of the activities you want to get done. Write each activity in a time slot on the homework chart. Choose a time that is best for you to study. If you like to take breaks between tasks, include breaks in your schedule. Be sure to include time for family, friends, chores, dinner, and recreation.

My Homework Chart

Time	Activity
3:00	
3:30	
4:00	
4:30	
5:00	
5:30	
6:00	
6:30	
7:00	
7:30	
8:00	
8:30	
9:00	

Name _____

Give Yourself a Break!

 **Take time to relax and carefully review instructions to avoid feeling frustrated.**

Have you ever looked at your homework and thought, "I can't do this?" When does this happen? Why do you feel frustrated? In the space below, write about subjects or assignments that frustrate you.

_____

_____

_____

Sometimes if you just take the time to relax and carefully review instructions, you can view the task from a different perspective. Listed below are some helpful hints for dealing with frustration.

- Reread the instructions.
- Reread the section in the book related to the assignment.
- Take a short break.
- Ask your teacher or your parent(s) for help.
- Use a sheet of paper to cover the assignment so you can only see the portion of the page you are working on.
- Divide the assignment into smaller, more manageable tasks and do one part at a time.

Circle the suggestion that you plan to try next time you feel frustrated.

Developing Effective Homework Habits

Helping Kids Get Organized © 1995 Good Apple

Name _____

Getting it There

 Leave your homework in a special place so that you won't forget to take it to school.

Some students have trouble keeping track of their homework. This can become a big problem because it's hard to get credit for an assignment that was left at home.

Answer each of the following questions and devise a plan to make sure you get your homework to school every day.

- Where do you usually do your homework?_____

- Where do you leave your homework when it doesn't get to school?

  _____

- Is there a special place where you leave things that you need to take to school the next day? Where is it?_____

- Where can you put your homework to make sure you take it to school with you?_____

- Can you leave time in the evening (maybe right before you go to bed) to gather what you need for school the next day? When?_____

Keep a record of the number of days in a row you remember to take your homework to school. Every day you remember, color one of the flags. When you miss a day, start over again and set a new record for yourself.

Name _____

Beat the Clock

 **Plan ahead for deadlines to keep from cramming at the last minute.**

One challenge many students face when they are completing projects is finishing before the deadline. It helps to start early and plan ahead. You usually don't do your best work when you must hurry.

Accurately estimating how long a task will take is a valuable skill. Estimate how long it takes you to do each of the following tasks. Then actually time yourself doing each task. Were your estimates correct?

Task	Estimated Time	Actual Time
Read a page from a book.		
Write three sentences.		
Complete an average math problem.		
Sharpen two pencils.		
Look up the word *chrysanthemum* in the dictionary.		

Dealing With Deadlines

Helping Kids Get Organized © 1995 Good Apple

Name _____

What's More Important?

 Use good judgment to determine which tasks should be done immediately and which ones can wait.

Prioritize the following activities by placing numbers next to them in order of importance. Use your best judgment.

____ Go to the toy store.

____ Play outside with your friends.

____ Attend baseball try-outs.

____ Complete a math assignment due tomorrow.

____ Watch television.

____ Begin research on a book report due in one week.

____ Help wash the dishes.

____ Finish reading a great book.

____ Clean your room.

____ Feed the dog.

____ Call your friends on the phone.

Explain why you set these priorities. Why did you choose your number one activity as most important? How did you choose which activity could be done last?

_____

_____

_____

_____

_____

Helping Kids Get Organized © 1995 Good Apple

Name _____

Set Your Own Priorities

 **Prioritize tasks so you know which ones are most important for meeting your deadlines.**

Some tasks are obviously more important than others. In the column on the left, list ten tasks you have to do this week. In the column on the right, rewrite the tasks in order of priority. Write the most important task at the top of the list and the task that is least important at the bottom of the list. Keep this list with you during the week. As you complete each task, cross it off your list.

_____

_____

_____

_____

_____

_____

_____

_____

_____

_____

1. _____

2. _____

3. _____

4. _____

5. _____

6. _____

7. _____

8. _____

9. _____

10. _____

Helping Kids Get Organized © 1995 Good Apple

Keeping Track

 Record and track your progress when you have a lot of material or books to read.

Use the graph to record the number of pages you read each day. Each time you do some reading, draw a vertical bar on the graph that starts at the correct day of the week and ends at the number of pages read. At the end of each week, add up all the pages and see how far you've progressed. This is a great way of finding out how long it takes you to complete a reading assignment so you can plan ahead for the next one.

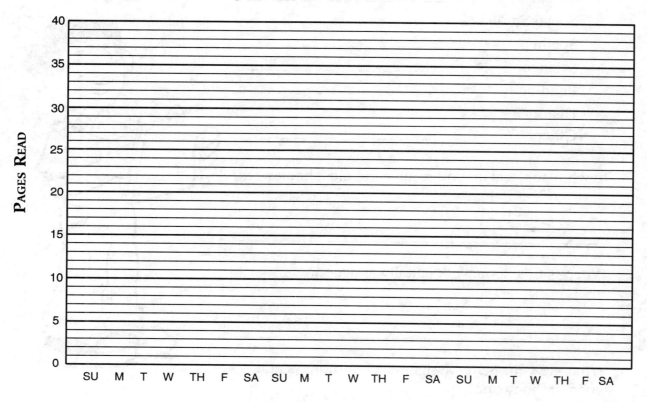

Make a list of the books you complete.

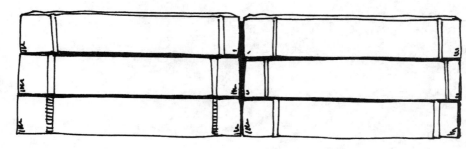

Name _____

Planning Your Week

 **Keep a weekly assignment sheet of what you must get done each day.**

Knowing when homework assignments are due and when tests are scheduled is crucial. Gather the following information to complete the Weekly Assignment Sheet.

On what day of the week do you usually have tests in these subjects?

Math _____

Social Studies _____

Spelling _____

Science _____

Reading _____

History _____

Others _____

In what subjects do you receive the most homework?

_____

_____

When is this homework usually assigned?

_____

_____

What are your major assignments or projects and when are they due?

_____

_____

Helping Kids Get Organized © 1995 Good Apple

Name _____

Weekly Assignment Sheet

Use this assignment sheet to keep track of your daily work load. Write your subjects on the left side and your daily assignments under the correct day of the week. Keep the assignment sheet in your desk and check it before leaving school every day to make sure you take home everything you need.

Week of _____

SUBJECTS	MONDAY	TUESDAY	WEDNESDAY	THURSDAY	FRIDAY
Math					

Dealing With Deadlines

Name _____

Order Counts

Determine the best order in which to complete each step of an assignment.

Sometimes you can make a task more difficult when you do it out of order. Order is particularly significant when you are doing long projects.

Read the tasks required to complete each project. Write a number from 1-6 beside each task to show in what order they should be done.

Write a Book Report

____ Proofread the report.

____ Select a book.

____ Type the final draft of the report.

____ Read the book.

____ Write a rough draft of the report.

____ Make a cover for the report.

Prepare a Meal

____ Sit down and eat.

____ Go to the grocery store.

____ Cook the food.

____ Set the table.

____ Decide what you are going to prepare.

____ Call everyone to dinner.

Plan for a Camping Trip

____ Pack your clothes and equipment.

____ Decide where you want to go.

____ Buy the equipment you need.

____ Gas up the car and you're on your way!

____ Collect several different vacation brochures.

____ Find someone to care for your pets while you're away.

Prioritizing Multiple Tasks

Helping Kids Get Organized © 1995 Good Apple

Name _____

Make it Manageable

 **Break major assignments into manageable parts to keep from feeling overwhelmed.**

Knowing how to break projects down and put them into the proper order will greatly enhance your feelings of accomplishment. What are the steps you need to take to complete the following projects? Break them down into manageable parts and put them in order.

Write a one-page report about Christopher Columbus. Consider gathering the information, taking notes, and completing the report.

1. _____
2. _____
3. _____
4. _____
5. _____

Construct a relief map of the state where you live. Consider the materials you would use, as well as what would be included on the map.

1. _____
2. _____
3. _____
4. _____
5. _____

Make a bowl of popcorn.

1. _____
2. _____
3. _____
4. _____
5. _____

Give a dog a bath.

1. _____
2. _____
3. _____
4. _____
5. _____

Prioritizing Multiple Tasks

Name _____

Ready, Set, Draw

Order is important in almost everything you do. In the space below, draw a picture of a person.

List the features in the order you drew them.

1. _____   6. _____
2. _____   7. _____
3. _____   8. _____
4. _____   9. _____
5. _____   10. _____

Draw another person. This time, draw the features you wrote beside the even numbers in your list (2, 4, 6, 8, 10) and then add the features you wrote beside the odd numbers (1, 3, 5, 7, 9).

Did you have any problems? Was it easier to draw the person the first time or the second time? Why?

_____

_____

Prioritizing Multiple Tasks

Name _____

Your Order Please!

 **Sequence is important in explaining directions clearly.**

Getting organized requires knowing the best way to accomplish a task. There's even an order for making a peanut butter and jelly sandwich. Explain the task to someone else by listing the necessary steps. Pretend you are writing directions for an alien who knows nothing about eating utensils, food, or sandwiches. When you are finished, invite a friend to follow your directions.

How to make a peanut butter and jelly sandwich.

1. _____
2. _____
3. _____
4. _____
5. _____
6. _____
7. _____
8. _____

Watch your friend follow your directions. Describe any problems he or she experienced while making the sandwich. What did you learn about writing directions?

_____

_____

_____

Now that you are a "pro" at giving directions, write directions for tying a shoelace.

1. _____
2. _____
3. _____
4. _____
5. _____

Name _____

Taking Steps

✏️ **Take small steps to reach large goals.**

Looking ahead to all the projects and tests you have to do throughout the year can be overwhelming. If you create order by prioritizing your assignments, you can accomplish these goals. Making a higher grade in a subject you are having trouble with may seem impossible at times, but you can do it if you set "teeny tiny" short-term goals for yourself.

Do you want to get an A in math? Would you like to be better at softball? Do you want to eat more nutritious meals or get in shape? Decide on three long-term goals that you would like to achieve. Think of the steps you can take to accomplish these goals without feeling overwhelmed. Make sure to be realistic and remember that order is important.

Long-Term Goal

_____

Steps I will take to get there

1. _____
2. _____
3. _____
4. _____
5. _____

Long-Term Goal

_____

Steps I will take to get there

1. _____
2. _____
3. _____
4. _____
5. _____

Long-Term Goal

_____

Steps I will take to get there

1. _____
2. _____
3. _____
4. _____
5. _____

Helping Kids Get Organized © 1995 Good Apple

Name _____

I Can Do it!

 **Set goals for success.**

To be successful, begin thinking of the goals you want to set for yourself. How can you do well in all your school subjects this year? Set a goal for each subject area and define at least two short-term goals that will help you reach it by the end of the month.

Math Goal

Short-term goal #1

Short-term goal #2

Science Goal

Short-term goal #1

Short-term goal #2

Writing Goal

Short-term goal #1

Short-term goal #2

Spelling Goal

Short-term goal #1

Short-term goal #2

Helping Kids Get Organized © 1995 Good Apple

Take a Picture

 Use your "mind's eye" to remember important information.

Memorizing is an important skill for retaining information. There are many different methods you can use to remember important details. Think of a new word that you learned this week. Take a picture of the word and its meaning with your mind. As you click the picture, observe it, spell it, and carefully envision what it means. Try to hold the image as if you were the camera and the word was a picture.

Once you've taken a picture, test your skill at remembering the word. Write the word and its definition down from memory.

_____

_____

Now, try your hand at remembering new words by using your "mind's eye." Each time you learn a new word this week, record it below. At the end of the week, see if you can still remember all of the words and their definitions.

Word	Definition
_____	_____
_____	_____
_____	_____
_____	_____
_____	_____

Name _____

Memories From My Past

 Practice remembering important events to exercise your mind.

There are always special events from your past that will stick in your mind. See how many special memories you can recall. Record your special memories and how old you were when the events happened.

My Special Memories

I remember when _____

_____

I was _____ years old.

I remember when _____

_____

I was _____ years old.

I remember when _____

_____

I was _____ years old.

Name _____

Picture This

Draw a picture of something new you
have learned to help you remember it.

Memories can be triggered in many different ways. Your five senses can
often lead you to remember things you had previously forgotten. You may
smell a flower that reminds you of a particular perfume. You may see a tree
or river that reminds you of a vacation you took last summer. Sight is often
the most important sense for triggering memories. Drawing a picture can
help you remember an important event or fact.

Write down four things you need to learn this week and then draw a picture
that will help you remember them.

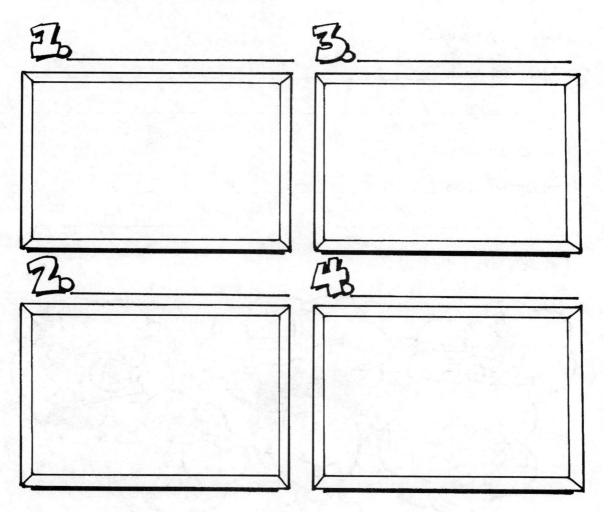

Helping Kids Get Organized © 1995 Good Apple

Name _____

Memory Makers

 Make up a silly sentence to help you remember important facts you need to know.

Memorizing takes time, but you can create ways that make it easier and more time efficient. Try to memorize each list below. Memorize the list of vegetables the way you usually memorize. Use a silly sentence to help you memorize the list of sports. Create a silly sentence in which each word begins with the first letter of a sport in the list. For example, "**T**wo **b**lue **g**orillas **s**at **f**acing **s**even **j**olly **r**hinos."

Vegetables
carrots
lettuce
eggplant
potatoes
squash
green beans
parsnips
brussel sprouts

Sports
tennis
baseball
gymnastics
soccer
football
swimming
jogging
racquetball

After one hour has passed, see if you can write both lists from memory on a separate sheet of paper.
How many vegetables did you remember? _____
How many sports did you remember? _____

Think of a silly sentence for each of the following lists so that you can remember them in the future.

Colors of the Rainbow
(violet, indigo, blue, green, yellow, orange, red)

_____

Planets in our Solar System
(Mercury, Venus, Earth, Mars, Jupiter, Saturn, Uranus, Neptune, Pluto)

_____

Name _____

Remember This Date

 **Devise a system for remembering the birthdays of your family and friends.**

Gather all the birthdates of your family and friends and list the dates below. Create a system that will help you remember the dates. For example, you can arrange the dates by month on index cards. You can file these cards or post each card where you will see it at the beginning of the appropriate month.

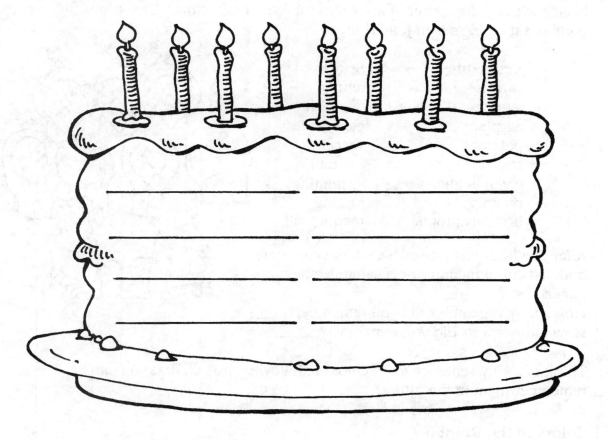

What is your strategy for remembering these birthdays?

_____

_____

Name _____

My Monthly Calendar

 Use a monthly calendar to look ahead to upcoming events and to remind you of special occasions you can plan for.

Fill in this month's calendar with the correct days and dates. List the activities, events, tests, and assignments you need to remember. Is there a project due? Are there tests you need to plan for? Do your friends or family have birthdays this month? Get in the habit of writing things down and watch how organized you will be.

SUNDAY	MONDAY	TUESDAY	WEDNESDAY	THURSDAY	FRIDAY	SATURDAY

The Body Scan

 **Each time you leave home, stop and look around the room to determine if you have everything you need.**

The body scan is a technique that will help you remember your belongings. Each time you leave home, use this method by asking yourself these questions.

- Do I have everything I need for school?
- Do I have my homework?
- Do I have my books, lunch, glasses, or coat?

Post this sign on your door or notebook to remind you to use the body scan technique so that you'll always have everything you need for school.

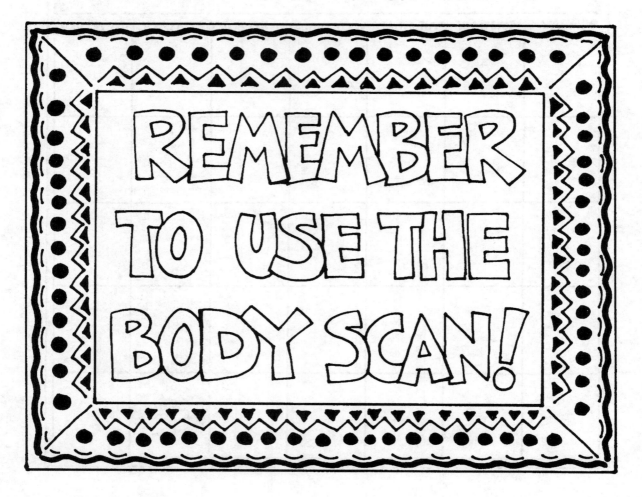

44

How Do I Begin?

 Develop a strategy for approaching major assignments.

Imagine that you have been asked to prepare and present an oral report on a famous person. This person can be a political figure, athlete, writer, movie star, or whoever captures your interest. Answer the questions below to identify and prioritize your strategy for completing the assignment.

1. Who is the person? _____

2. For what is he or she famous? _____

3. Where will you find information about this famous person? _____

_____

4. Where can you go to get these resources? _____

5. How will you know which pieces of information to include in the report?

_____

_____

6. If your oral presentation is to last five minutes, how long should your written report be? _____

7. Will you use sheets of paper or note cards when presenting your report? Why? _____

8. How should you record the information before completing the final report? _____

_____

Writing Reports: Research and Organization

The Main Idea

 Remember that every well written paragraph has one main idea.

Authors try to convey information as clearly as possible. Books are divided into chapters, chapters are divided into paragraphs, and paragraphs are divided into sentences. Each paragraph conveys a particular idea. As you read, look for the main ideas the author is trying to express. For each paragraph below, write one sentence that describes the main idea the author is presenting.

Richard Nixon was the 37th president of the United States and the only president to resign from office. He left office on August 9, 1974. If he had remained in office, he probably would have faced impeachment for his role in the Watergate scandal.

The Watergate scandal began with the burglary of the offices of the Democratic party in the Watergate office complex. This was only a portion of the illegal activities that were conducted by employees of President Nixon's reelection staff. Nixon and his staff tried to cover up these activities.

President Nixon is also remembered for many other important events during his presidency. It was during his presidency that the Vietnam War ended and the military draft was eliminated. President Nixon also opened diplomatic relations with China.

What is the main idea of each paragraph above?

1. _____
_____
_____

2. _____
_____
_____
_____

3. _____
_____
_____

Writing Reports: Research and Organization

Helping Kids Get Organized © 1995 Good Apple

The Book Knows the Answer

 Become familiar with your textbooks so you can find information quickly and easily.

Do you know how to find all the information available to you in your textbooks? Turn to each of the following sections of your social studies or history book and identify the kinds of information found in these sections.

Table of Contents _____

_____

Index _____

_____

Glossary _____

_____

Chapter Introduction _____

_____

References _____

_____

Where might you look if you wanted to find other books on subjects covered in this book?_____

What would be the quickest way to find more information about a person you read about in your textbook? _____

If you need to know how to pronounce a word introduced in the text, where would you look? _____

If you were looking at a new book and wanted to get an idea of the topics included in the text, where would you look? _____

Helping Kids Get Organized © 1995 Good Apple

Name _____

Notes and More Notes

 **Keep track of your sources and give credit for the information you collect.**

Sometimes you must use a number of sources to get information for a report. When you are taking notes from a number of reference materials, keep track of the notes and sources with the following system.

• Use a 3" x 5" card for each reference source.

• In the top right hand corner of each card, identify the reference source with a letter of the alphabet.

• Write the author, title of book, publisher, and copyright date on the card.

• Each time you take notes from a source, write them on a 3" x 5" card with the identifying letter of the book in the top right-hand corner. Number the note cards in consecutive order, such as A1, A2, A3.

• Always paraphrase or write the notes in your own words. Never copy directly from the text unless you plan to give credit to the author.

• If you want to quote directly from the book, write down the words exactly as they are printed and place quotation marks around them.

• Always identify the page number on which you found your information. This way, you will be able to footnote quoted material in your report with the source and page number.

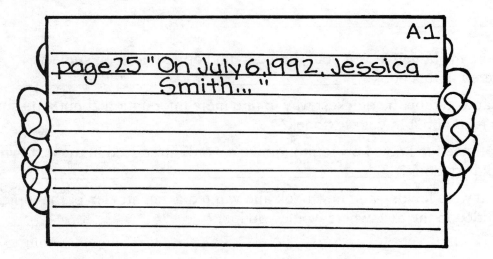

page 25 "On July 6, 1992, Jessica Smith..."

Writing Reports: Research and Organization

Proofreading Principles

 **Proofread every written assignment for spelling, punctuation, and grammatical errors.**

You've worked very hard to write a good report. The content is excellent but you forgot to proofread your assignment. Next time, remember these proofreading principles.

Step 1
Proofread for spelling the first time through. Read the work silently, looking at each word carefully for spelling alone. If you have difficulty simply looking for spelling errors, read your work backwards.

Step 2
Reread your work aloud. This time, listen for grammatical errors, sentence structure, and the flow of ideas.

Step 3
Make sure every sentence is a complete sentence, beginning with a capital letter and ending with a period.

Review your last two book reports or written assignments and answer these questions.

How many errors did you find?_____

How many punctuation errors did you find? _____

How many spelling errors did you find?_____

What kind of errors do you make most often?_____

What could you have done to prevent most of your errors? How will you prevent them in the future?

_____

_____

Name _____

Put on Your Proofer's Cap

 **Practice proofreading skills by looking over old assignments.**

Proofread the work below using what you've learned. Find and circle the errors.

Learning how to study is a important skill. Once learned, it will help you all your life, weather you are in elementary school, middle school, high school, or college. many very good student have a difficult time in college because they newer learned how to study.

Learning how to use your time efficiently is especially important. You may study a chapter in your science book for hours, but that will be of little use unless you spend your time wizely.

The title and headings of a chapter hold valuable information. Before reading chapter, skim through it's contents. What the major chapter headings? What pictures, graphs, or charts did you find. Are where any special vocabulary words you should know? Before reading the chapter, note several questions that you think the chapter will answer. Read the chapter with these question in mind. After reading the chapter, answer the questions you posed. What other important information, did you learn in the chapter?

Did you find all thirteen errors? If you didn't, go back and see if you can find the errors you missed.

Writing Reports: Research and Organization

Helping Kids Get Organized © 1995 Good Apple

Name _____

The Right References

Know which reference books contain the information you need for your assignments.

There are a lot of reference books designed to provide just the kind of information you are looking for. Match these books with the types of information they provide.

Thesaurus _____

Atlas _____

Dictionary _____

Almanac _____

Bartlett's *Familiar Quotations* _____

Unabridged Dictionary _____

Relief Map _____

Encyclopedia _____

Style Manual _____

a. Synonyms and antonyms
b. Rules for grammar, punctuation, typing, and writing papers
c. Most comprehensive dictionary
d. Map showing topography and differences in elevation
e. Annually published book of interesting facts about countries, the calendar year, events such as tides, sunrise and sunset, and sports facts
f. Quotations from a variety of sources, including famous people and well-known written works
g. Book of maps
h. Book or set of books containing information on various topics arranged in alphabetical order
i. Words, their pronunciation, spelling, and definitions

Look in your school or local library and find three other kinds of reference books not listed here and include the type of information they provide.

1. _____

2. _____

3. _____

Name _____

Find it Fast

 **Learn how to use a dictionary as one of your most valuable resources.**

It's important to know how to use a dictionary. Here are some simple ways of finding the information you need as quickly as possible.

• To practice opening the dictionary to the approximate location of a word, play the "ABC Game." This is a game for two players. One player names a letter of the alphabet. The other player tries to open the dictionary to a page with words beginning with that letter. Wherever the dictionary is opened, count how many letters away from the goal letter you are. For example, if you are looking for the letter *D* and you open the dictionary to the letter *G* (which is three letters away), you would accumulate three points. The person with the fewest points wins the game.

• At the top of each page of the dictionary you will find two words called *guide words*. The first guide word tells you what word is first on the page. The second guide word tells you what word is last on the page. Use guide words to help you locate a word in the dictionary.

What are the guide words on the page of the dictionary containing these words?

hostile   _____

               _____

study   _____

               _____

dictionary   _____

               _____

automobile _____

               _____

constant   _____

               _____

            Writing Reports: Research and Organization

Helping Kids Get Organized © 1995 Good Apple

Check Up on Study Skills

> ▭▷ **Turn good study skills into good habits.**

How many of these suggestions do you follow when you study for a test? As you read the list below, check off the things you do before a test. Are there other items listed here that you could incorporate into your study habits? Use this list as a study guide for your next test.

☐ 1. Plan ahead so that you do not have to cram at the last minute.

☐ 2. Give yourself plenty of time to read assignments more than once.

☐ 3. Before reading, look over the major headings and subheadings of the chapter to remind yourself what the chapter is about.

☐ 4. Pose questions that you will answer by reading the chapter.

☐ 5. If you own the book, underline or highlight the important ideas in each chapter.

☐ 6. If you cannot write in the book, take notes of the main ideas described in each chapter.

☐ 7. Read each section once, then reread the underlined portions of your notes to reinforce the information in your memory.

☐ 8. After reading a section, repeat the important points aloud.

☐ 9. Make a mock test for yourself or exchange mock tests with a classmate.

☐ 10. Find a study partner and quiz each other on the most important points from the material.

Everyone has special skills and practices that they develop to help them study. List some of yours and share them with your classmates.

_____

_____

_____

_____

Name _____

Best Test Planner

> ✏️ **Before a test, write down the most important information from the material you've been studying and keep it organized.**

Use this test planner to help you prepare for an upcoming test.

Test Subject _____ **Test Date** _____

Test Type (multiple-choice, short answer, essay, true-false)

_____

What will this test cover?	What specific information do I need to study?
_____ _____ _____ _____	_____ _____ _____ _____
What materials do I need to bring home?	How will I quiz myself?
_____ _____ _____ _____	_____ _____ _____ _____

Helping Kids Get Organized © 1995 Good Apple

Name _____

It's Okay to Ask

 **Ask questions to help you understand information more clearly.**

Successful students ask questions. Are you ever afraid to ask a question because you think someone may laugh at you? Remember, no question is ever too silly to ask. Here are some tips for asking questions.

- **Know *Who* to Ask**

  Who would you ask . . .

  To help you find a book? _____

  To help you complete a math problem? _____

  If you may stay after school to work on an assignment? _____

  To find out what you are having for dinner? _____

- **Know *How* and *When* to Ask a Question**

  Raise your hand and wait to be called on when you ask a question in class.

  Write down your questions so that you will remember them when you have the opportunity to ask.

  Listen carefully to the answer.

Write a question to go with each of these answers.

Q: _____

A: 50 states

Q: _____

A: 12 inches

Q: _____

A: verb

Helping Kids Get Organized © 1995 Good Apple

Name _____

Super Study Method

 Use the SQ3R method to study more effectively and target the most important points from your reading material.

SQ3R is a study technique that has been around for a long time. Taking the time to learn and use it will greatly increase your chances of academic success. SQ3R stands for **S**urvey, **Q**uestion, **R**ead, **R**ecite, and **R**eview.

Survey
Before you begin reading a chapter or unit of text, survey the pages. Look at chapter headings, special vocabulary, diagrams, and pictures.

Question
Write down several questions you think you will be able to answer after reading the material.

Read
Read the material to find the answers to your questions.

Recite
When you find an answer to one of your questions, recite the answer aloud.

Review
After reading the material, review what you have read by looking over the material again and writing down the answers to each of your questions.

Helping Kids Get Organized © 1995 Good Apple

Using SQ3R

 **Practice the SQ3R method to develop valuable reading skills.**

Choose one of your reading assignments to test the SQ3R method. Answer the following questions as you use the SQ3R method.

1. What is the chapter title and what are the major headings?

_____

_____

_____

2. Write down several questions you think the information in the chapter will answer.

_____

_____

_____

3. Read the assigned material and look for the answers to your questions.

4. Did you find all the answers to your questions? _____

5. How did the SQ3R method work for you? In what ways did you find it helpful?

_____

_____

_____

Name _____

Test it Out

Be a successful test-taker by knowing the information on which you are being tested and understanding how to take the test.

Make a check mark next to each test-taking tip that you have used.

☐ 1. Make sure you have all materials you need before coming to the test, including extra pencils and batteries for calculators.

☐ 2. Read all the directions for the test before beginning. Know how you must show your answer. Do you circle it, underline it, or write a complete answer?

☐ 3. If the test calls for all answers to be written in complete sentences, restate the question as you answer it.
  Q: Who was the first president of the United States?
  A: The first president of the United States was . . .

☐ 4. When taking a math test, find out whether you must show your work or if you can use scrap paper.

☐ 5. On a math test, put a small dot under each problem to show that you have checked your work.

☐ 6. If the test is multiple-choice, answer all the questions you know first and then go back to the questions you are less sure of.

☐ 7. On a multiple-choice question, rule out all the possibilities that you know are wrong. Then, decide between those answers that seem probable.

☐ 8. Relax and take your time.

☐ 9. Focus on your own work and not the work of those around you.

☐ 10. Make sure your answers are written neatly and legibly.

☐ 11. When you are taking a true-false test, watch carefully for words like *never, always, all,* and *only.* Often these words will make a statement false.

☐ 12. When taking an essay test, organize the information you write so that you can show you have a good understanding of the material.

How many of these test-taking tips have you used? _____

Which new test-taking tips are you planning to use for your next test?

_____

_____

Follow Your Nose

 **Always read directions thoroughly before beginning an assignment.**

Have you ever taken a test only to realize that you answered questions incorrectly because you failed to read the directions carefully? Directions will not only tell you what information is needed in the answer, but also in what form the answer should appear.

Complete the following assignment. Read the entire page, following all directions.

1. Write the numbers from 1 to 100 backwards.

2. Write ten words that begin with the letter *A*. Write the same ten words again in alphabetical order.

1. _____	1. _____
2. _____	2. _____
3. _____	3. _____
4. _____	4. _____
5. _____	5. _____
6. _____	6. _____
7. _____	7. _____
8. _____	8. _____
9. _____	9. _____
10. _____	10. _____

3. Write a paragraph introducing yourself to the class. Include information about your family, your likes and dislikes, favorite school subject, and anything else that makes you special.

4. Do not complete #1, #2, or #3. Pat yourself on the back for following the directions and reading the entire page before beginning your work.

What's in a Question?

 **Underline specific directions and assignment questions before beginning a task.**

Often students complete an assignment, but don't answer the questions correctly because they did not follow directions. Make sure your work answers the questions asked.

For each task, underline specific directions and the question that must be answered. List any materials, supplies, or references you will need for the task. Then define what you will do to answer the question. (You do not need to actually answer the questions. Just prepare to answer them.)

Example
14% of the human body is made of muscles. <u>How much do the muscles in your body weigh?</u>

Materials: Scale, pencil, and paper
To do this task, I must weigh myself and then multiply .14 by my body weight.

1. Bernie wanted to open a lawn mowing business. He borrowed $100 to purchase a used lawn mower. If he charges $10 an hour to mow lawns, how many hours will he have to work before he makes a profit?
Materials: _____

Task: _____

2. Draw a picture of the original flag of the United States of America. How many stars are on it?
Materials: _____

Task: _____

3. Suzanne wants to make a new tablecloth for her table. The fabric she has selected costs $5.95 a yard and is 60 inches wide. How much will the tablecloth cost if she buys 5 yards of fabric?
Materials: _____

Task: _____

Helping Kids Get Organized © 1995 Good Apple

Check Your Work

 **Circle the operation signs when completing math problems.**

One of the most common errors in math is using the wrong operation to get the answer. This is a common mistake that is easily corrected.

In the problems below, circle the operation sign. Then, circle the problems that are incorrect because the wrong operation was used.

$$
\begin{array}{r} 22 \\ \times 7 \\ \hline 154 \end{array}
\qquad
\begin{array}{r} 634 \\ +88 \\ \hline 722 \end{array}
\qquad
\begin{array}{r} 72 \\ -33 \\ \hline 105 \end{array}
$$

$$
\begin{array}{r} 1819 \\ +712 \\ \hline 2531 \end{array}
\qquad
\begin{array}{r} 2660 \\ -320 \\ \hline 2980 \end{array}
\qquad
\begin{array}{r} 331 \\ +661 \\ \hline 992 \end{array}
$$

Look over your math homework and test sheets. How many times have you made this kind of error?

Helping Kids Get Organized © 1995 Good Apple

Developing Test-Taking Skills

Math Checks

 **Always check your work after completing a math assignment.**

Check each problem in the test below by doing the reciprocal problem. For example, if the problem involves addition, the reciprocal problem would be to subtract one addend from the sum. If the addition problem was done correctly, the answer to the subtraction problem will be the other addend.

```
  233        Check
 +233
  466
```

```
  456        Check
 -201
  255
```

```
   22        Check
  x16
  352
```

```
     22      Check
 10)220
```

Helping Kids Get Organized © 1995 Good Apple

Name _____

Long-Term Assignments

 Use a chart or planning sheet to keep track of your progress on long-term assignments.

Sometimes your assignments will take several days or weeks to complete. You may have individual and group projects as well as term papers that require more than a few days to finish. Planning ahead is the key to getting these projects done.

Do you have any monthly assignments, such as book reports? What are they?_____

Do you have any weekly assignments, such as bringing in a current event newspaper article? _____

Do you have any after-school activities, such as band practice or sports which require extended practice sessions? What are they?

_____

_____

Have you been assigned a major project, such as a term paper, class presentation, or science project? Describe it.

_____

_____

Describe your style for completing long-term assignments. Do you start the assignment long before it is due? Do you break the assignment down into manageable parts? Do you wait until the last minute?

_____

_____

Keep track of long-term assignments with a calendar. Use the Long-Term Assignment Planning Sheet to keep track of your progress on your next major project.

Name _____

Long-Term Assignment Planning Sheet

Assignment: _____

_____

Due Date: _____

TASK	DUE DATE	COMPLETED
Step 1		
Step 2		
Step 3		

Planning for Long-Term Projects

Name _____

Using Your Head to Plan Ahead

 **Plan ahead to complete major projects and long-term assignments on time.**

Has an assignment ever crept up on you? You knew about the assignment well in advance but somehow, before you realized it, the due date was upon you. Here are some questions to ask yourself when planning ahead for a long-term assignment.

What is the assignment?
____ Test
____ Paper
____ Project
____ Oral Report
____ Other_____

What is the due date? _____

How long is that from now? _____

What kind of research is required for the project?

_____

Will I be working by myself or in a group?

_____

What skills and tasks will be involved in completing this assignment?

____ Time management
____ Locating information
____ Reading
____ Taking notes
____ Writing rough draft
____ Creating media materials, such as a poster, diorama, or display
____ Writing final report
____ Practicing and presenting oral report

Name _____

Ahead of the Game

 **Understand what an assignment involves so you can make a reasonable plan for completing it on time.**

Use "My Assignment Calendar" to plan for your next project. If you have more than one month to work on your project, copy the calendar and fill it in for each month you will be working. Design a reasonable course of action using these suggestions.

1. Consider the tasks included in your assignment.

2. Estimate how long it will take you to locate materials, read, take notes, write a rough draft, and so on. Allow yourself a certain amount of time for each task. List each task and the estimated time.

3. Mark the due date for your assignment with a large red X. Mark the half-way point with a blue X.

4. Counting back from the due date, mark each assignment task on the calendar.

5. As you complete each task, mark it out with a green X on the calendar.

6. When you reach the blue X, check to see if you are on time with your tasks.

7. If you are keeping up with your tasks, reward yourself for staying on time. If you are not keeping up, work a bit harder to get back on track.

Helping Kids Get Organized © 1995 Good Apple

Name _____

My Assignment Calendar

MONTH OF _____

SUNDAY	MONDAY	TUESDAY	WEDNESDAY	THURSDAY	FRIDAY	SATURDAY

Step by Step

 **Learn the difference between realistic and unrealistic goals.**

Have you ever been so frustrated by a task that you wanted to give up? Sometimes we expect too much of ourselves too quickly. Think about a tightrope walker. How did he or she learn to walk across the high wire? First steps are taken on a wire laid on the ground. Next, a short wire may be suspended a few inches above the ground. When the tightrope walker becomes more confident, the wire is lengthened. As he or she gains proficiency, the distance between safe stopping points is lengthened and the wire is raised higher above the ground. Learning a skill, studying a topic, or completing an assignment requires the same step-by-step approach.

First, the goals you set for yourself must be realistic and attainable. Which goals listed below are realistic for you? Circle the goals that you think you could achieve.

1. I will eat 250 marshmallows for dinner tonight.

2. I can read 10 pages of my book before bedtime.

3. I will pitch at an Atlanta Braves baseball game.

4. I will remember to take my homework to school each day this week.

5. I will go to a movie every day for a year.

6. I can eat my weight in strawberries.

7. I will make an A in every subject this year.

8. I can bring up my grades in math by five points.

9. I will make a B on my next language arts assignment.

10. I can walk one mile three times this week.

Helping Kids Get Organized © 1995 Good Apple

Name _____

Realistic Goals

 **Set realistic and manageable goals for yourself.**

Now that you understand the difference between realistic and unrealistic, you can begin to set some realistic goals for yourself. Goals can be set for any area of your life. What are some realistic goals that you have for yourself in each of the following areas? (Use this activity to help you with *Short-Term vs. Long-Term Goals* on page 70.)

Reading

1. _____

_____

2. _____

_____

Sports/Fitness

1. _____

_____

2. _____

_____

Math

1. _____

_____

2. _____

_____

Friends

1. _____

_____

2. _____

_____

Family

1. _____

_____

2. _____

_____

Nutrition

1. _____

_____

2. _____

_____

Name _____

Short-Term vs. Long-Term Goals

Set short-term goals along the way as you work towards reaching a long-term goal.

Some goals are easily and quickly accomplished. These are called *short-term goals*. Goals that take a long time and a lot of hard work to achieve are called *long-term goals*. Mark each goal as short-term (S) or long-term (L).

—— 1. Read 10 books.

—— 2. Read 1 book.

—— 3. Save some money from my allowance.

—— 4. Earn $100.

—— 5. Get all A's on my report card.

—— 6. Earn a score of 85 on this week's spelling test.

Look at the "realistic goals" you set for yourself on page 69. Write the goals below and label each as a long-term or short-term goal.

Reading

1._____

This is a _____ goal

2._____

This is a _____ goal

Sports/Fitness

1._____

This is a _____ goal

2._____

This is a _____ goal

Math

1._____

This is a _____ goal

2._____

This is a _____ goal

Friends

1._____

This is a _____ goal

2._____

This is a _____ goal

Family

1._____

This is a _____ goal

2._____

This is a _____ goal

Nutrition

1._____

This is a _____ goal

2._____

This is a _____ goal

Helping Kids Get Organized © 1995 Good Apple

Name _____

Moving Toward Your Goal

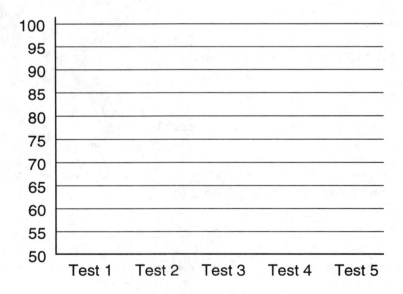

✏️ **Chart and keep track of your goals.**

Sometimes by simply keeping track of a goal, you can reach it. By achieving short-term goals along the way, you will reach your ultimate goal before you know it. Pick a school subject in which you would like to improve. Set a realistic long-term goal for yourself in this subject. Set three short-term goals that will help you reach the long-term goal. Plot your test grades on the graph and see if you can achieve your goal.

Long-Term Goal _____

Short-term goal #1 _____

Short-term goal #2 _____

Short-term goal #3 _____

```
100 ─────────────────────────────────────
 95 ─────────────────────────────────────
 90 ─────────────────────────────────────
 85 ─────────────────────────────────────
 80 ─────────────────────────────────────
 75 ─────────────────────────────────────
 70 ─────────────────────────────────────
 65 ─────────────────────────────────────
 60 ─────────────────────────────────────
 55 ─────────────────────────────────────
 50 ─────────────────────────────────────
     Test 1   Test 2   Test 3   Test 4   Test 5
```

My first five test scores averaged _____

My grade on my first report card _____

Name _____

Reach for the Sky

 **Be diligent about working hard to achieve your goals.**

There are many famous people who have set and achieved high goals through hard work and dedication. Some of these are politicians, athletes, writers, actors/actresses, and scientists. Is there someone you admire and wish you were more like?

Think of someone you admire. It could be a famous person like those listed above or it could be a friend, teacher, or parent. In the space below, write who this person is and what steps you could take to achieve some of the same goals he or she did.

I admire _____

because _____

_____

Steps I could take to achieve similar goals

_____

_____

_____

Write a long-term "Reach for the Sky" goal for:

School _____

_____

Career _____

_____

Family _____

_____

Friends _____

_____

Setting and Achieving Academic Goals

Helping Kids Get Organized © 1995 Good Apple

Look Whoooo's Organized

Use this bulletin board idea to reinforce and reward students' organizational progress. Duplicate an owl for each student and write his or her name on it. Display the owls on a bulletin board titled, "Look Whoooo's Organized." Each time a student hands in organized papers, homework, or displays good organizational skills, place a small gold star on that student's owl.

Pats on the Back for Organized Kids

COUNT ON ME

Congratulations! You are a student who can be counted on to be organized and get work done! Each time you are organized, do your work neatly, or complete an assignment on time, write what you did on one of the stars. Be proud of yourself for doing such a great job.

Pats on the Back for Organized Kids

Helping Kids Get Organized © 1995 Good Apple

CLUTTER CONTROL AWARD

The Clutter Control has recognized

_____
student

for doing an outstanding job of keeping things organized!
Keep up the good work!

_____
teacher

CLEAN DESK AWARD

The Clean Desk Award is given to

_____
student

for keeping a clean, neat and organized desk.

You set a great example!

_____
teacher

Helping Kids Get Organized © 1995 Good Apple

Pats on the Back for Organized Kids

ORGANIZATION AWARD
Thank you!

_____
student

Your outstanding job of being organized
has helped to prepare you for school!
Your hard work is noticed and
appreciated.

_____
teacher

LOOK WHO'S ON A ROLL!

_____
student

is on the ball and organized!
Congratulations!

_____
teacher

Pats on the Back for Organized Kids

Helping Kids Get Organized © 1995 Good Apple

SEAL OF APPROVAL

_____
student

is completely organized
and that is terrific!

_____
teacher

_____
student

**is totally organized and on the right track!
Congratulations!**

_____
teacher

Pats on the Back for Organized Kids

STAR STUDENT MAKES PROGRESS

_____
student

makes organizational headlines by organizing desk, homework, and papers.

Congratulations!

IMPORTANT ADVANCEMENT

_____
student

has made a huge advancement in getting organized.

This is terrific news!

Pats on the Back for Organized Kids

Note These!

student _____

Please work harder at getting the following organized. I know you can do it!

_____

_____

_____

Please have your work ready by _____

teacher _____

ORGANIZATIONAL TIPS

_____
student

Here are some organizational tips!

_____

_____

_____

_____

teacher _____

PUT US TO THE TEST

Reserve this date _____

for a test in _____

Start getting prepared now!

_____   _____
student   parent

This is a Test

Are you ready for a test in _____ ?

The test date is _____

Be sure to prepare yourself!

_____   _____
student   parent